No One Ever Told Me That

227 Tips for
School Business Administrators

Ted Witt

pretty
road
press

Published by Pretty Road Press
in partnership with the
California Association of School Business Officials

Pretty Road Press
P.O. Box 273
Folsom, California 95763-0273
www.PrettyRoadPress.com

Smart business. Smart schools.™

California Association of School Business Officials
1001 K Street, 5th Floor
Sacramento, CA 95814

Published 2012
Printed in the United States of America

15 14 13 12   5 4 3 2

ISBN 978-0-9826014-1-9

We salute Ted Witt and appreciate his dedication to CASBO and the profession of school business. Ted served as CASBO's executive director and was instrumental in the early development of our association. He has continued to be a strong supporter and proponent of professionalism and leadership in all areas of public education. We welcome this book and our continued partnership. We hope that the wisdom of this book will propel you forward in your career.

Molly McGee Hewitt, CAE
CASBO Executive Director

Contents

Hiring New Employees

It's time to hire a new employee. Of course you won't take this task lightly, but have you thoroughly mapped out the desired skills, as well as personal characteristics, of the employee you seek? The more preparation invested in the hiring process, the more likely you will find yourself a person who will benefit your team for the long term. Prepare less, expect less.

1. Start with your job description and profile outline.
The job description is the obvious part. You already know the job duties and the required skills. But what profile are you seeking? An employee who can get along with coworkers? A person who can make independent decisions? A candidate who can tolerate ambiguity?

Chances are these attributes are not written down. Make a list. Use this list in the development of questions.

2. Review the interview evaluation instrument.
Does the evaluation instrument measure all aspects of the job description, plus the profile characteristics you identified? Work with the personnel office to retool the instrument and to make sure you will not be asking questions that violate privacy or civil rights laws.
It should be simple enough for you to immediately determine and rank whether the candidate possesses the skills, experiences or profile you are looking for. Weight the evaluation area for the most important skills and characteristics.

3. Build a bank of questions within each evaluation area.
You must build a bank of questions related to each area to be evaluated, which may include experience, honesty, creativity, technical knowledge, human relations, or leadership. Fill your bank with at least four questions in each area. Some will be thrown out, others retooled. You can save questions for another interview. You may need more questions in one area than another. The number one reason why people are not successful in a job is their inability to get along with others. Use as many questions

as you need to get the desired information. The best questions can cross over into several evaluation areas.

4. Don't ask the obvious.

Don't waste your time seeking information from the applicant that you can get elsewhere. It may not be necessary for a person to reiterate all previous jobs. They are listed on the resume. Instead, ask a more pointed question. For example, "How do you think your experience in making budget cuts will help us when we are, instead of lacking money, well funded?

5. Recast your bank of questions in a variety of forms.

Use a little creativity. Avoid questions that require a yes or no answer. You can ask situational questions. Ask catalog questions that require a person to list specifically what they did on a given day at their current job. Ask questions that require people to use their imagination. Think about using these words and phrases in your questions: *describe, what if, define, if you could, role play, imagine, persuade me, distinguish between, what would you do if, tell me about,* and *convince me*.

6. Ask, listen and observe.

Interview panels often spend too much time asking and talking. Ask and then listen intently. Don't worry about the next question or who is asking it. Listen to the candidate. Look for behaviors that may impact the job. Some candidates purposely get you to talk so they can use the information to determine their answers. If an answer is short, don't jump in with a follow-up question. Judge how a candidate reacts to silence. Your observations of behavior are as important as the oral answers.

Navigating Office Politics

Every office has politics, but the political rules are never written down. Politics are about relationships and how they are used to accomplish an agenda. The politics in your office are likely to fall in your favor, if you heed these tips.

1. Be ethical.
No matter what, heed the ethical voice you have inside. It's paramount. Violate your ethical standards and you will always lose in the political game – maybe not immediately, but eventually you will lose. By maintaining your standards, you may make some colleagues temporarily uncomfortable, but violate your ethics and you will make permanent enemies. Do your

own job well. Respect ultimately earns you more points in the office's political game.

2. Be cooperative, both to the meek and to the mighty.

When asked for a favor, try to oblige, regardless of the status or title of the asking party. Speed things up. Break through the bureaucracy. If the answer has to be no, because of policy, ethics, or good business, then explore alternatives. Know the person's goals. If necessary, help individuals find another, more reasonable route to their objectives. In the long run, you will earn more respect in your office by serving the clerk and your customers as well as you serve the superintendent and the board member.

3. Practice empathy without gossip.

The most astute leaders know how to engage in conversation, listen to employees and hear concerns without participating in gossip. They don't reveal personal information, disclose embarrassing details, backbite or dwell on negatives. Instead, successful leaders express understanding of concerns, avoid emotional responses, and focus on solutions to difficult issues arising out of personality conflicts, relationships and work habits.

4. Be proactive with your boss.

Develop an open, honest relationship with your boss. Are you carrying old resentments? If you have had a difficult relationship, start anew today with a personal compliment. Find a way to praise your boss in front of others. Express concerns over policy and decisions alone with your boss – before they come up in public settings. Support your supervisor in meetings. Never personally criticize your boss to other employees; he or she will hear about it. Your responsibility is to bring a concern or criticism to your supervisor's attention. You will build trust, and the political winds will blow in your favor.

5. Be visible.

You may think the holiday luncheon is a waste of time. You're wrong. People matter. Be where people are. Attend board meetings, and make sure you also spend time in the lunch room with the clerks, the supervisors and the professionals. You will learn as much there as in the board room. Take the initiative to introduce yourself to people you do not know. Find a way to memorize their names. Remember them. Not only will they be impressed, you will find the information helpful to you in your future work. People have a hard time disliking a person who has taken the time to be genuinely friendly.

6. Be careful with your power.

You have now taken five steps to improve your position in office politics. People are eager to please you and help you. You are in a key position to use politics to influence a decision or make something happen. Go back to tip number one. Ensure that your decisions are not self-serving. Instead, use your political power to sway opinions and decisions in favor of students and stakeholders. It only takes one self-serving use of your powerful political juices to sour colleagues and jeopardize a respected reputation.

Improving Your Decisions

D o you readily make decisions, or do you agonize over each little detail? Are some decisions easier than others? Whether you find decisions easy or difficult, you may still be basing your decisions on the wrong factors. Review the following tips to assess your decision making abilities.

1. Don't center your decision making on a bad anchor.

An anchor is akin to an initial bad assumption. Anchors become established when people mention a fact or figure out of context or without doing their homework. For example, "How much more than $40 million in bonds can we expect the voters to approve?" A committee might answer, "$45 million or $50 million." In fact, the problem may necessitate an issue of $150 million in bonds, but because of the anchor, the decision-making process centers on the lower number. Opinion polls are infamous for creating anchors. Sometimes an anchor is created on purpose to frame an issue. For instance, anchoring is a common and deliberate ploy in many series of negotiations.

2. Beware of confirming advice.

You have a hunch about what decision you want to make, but you'd feel better going to some trusted colleagues and asking their advice. You may be setting up a situation in which you simply get confirming information. The problem is that you may ask leading questions or paint the nature of the problem with a bias toward your thinking. Lay out all facts, even those that seem to fly in the face of your hunch. Urge your colleague to play the devil's advocate and seek out some contrarians as well as some confidants.

3. When prudent, forsake the status quo.

The status quo often becomes the de facto decision because it's safe and known, and managers don't have the courage to shake things up. But, based on numbers and potential results, the status quo is often the wrong decision. Experiments show that when confronted with the choice of the status quo and two new alternatives, decision makers most often choose the status quo. Why? It's too difficult to decide between the two new alternatives.

4. Don't throw good money after bad.

We all deny that we would ever do this, but it is a natural human reaction. Say you invest $10,000 to repair a district office air conditioner. It breaks again three weeks later. It will take $20,000 to repair the second time around, and experts predict the system will have a maximum life of 18 more months. You elect to spend $20,000 because you don't want to appear to have wasted the $10,000 you spent earlier. Wrong decision. Get out of this trap by pretending that the first repair was made at no cost. Now, does it make sense to spend $20,000 for 18 months or should you totally replace the system? Those will be the answers on which to base a good decision.

5. Distinguish coincidence from true patterns.

Just because a coin flips to heads five times in a row does not mean that it will land heads on the sixth toss. Random chance is random chance. Many decisions are made on events that are coincidental and not true patterns. One Monday morning five new kindergartners arrive on your doorstep from three different private schools. Is there a causal pattern or is it coincidence?

Test your theories against historical data and experience. When events are truly random, don't even try to outguess chance. Gamblers will always lose in the end.

6. Don't base your decisions on one day's headlines.

It's a fact that publicity of dramatic events affects your recall of events in a formidable way. The reporting of two school shootings within the span of two weeks will evoke the impression that school violence is on the rise. Maybe it is, but you can't tell based on the reporting of those two events. Maybe you've heard horror stories of a computer conversion in one district. Do you know the success in others and have you isolated the reasons for the catastrophe in the original case? Whenever you make a decision, don't trust your recollection of headline news or gossip. Get real facts and figures. Isolate the variables and make an informed decision.

7. Discover your hidden assumptions.

Mary is either a teacher or an accountant. Her personnel evaluation describes her as a detail-oriented person. What are the chances she is an accountant? If you gave better than 50 percent odds that Mary is an accountant, explore your propensity to depend on hidden assumptions. In fact, the odds are well in favor of Mary being a teacher, since there are hundreds more teachers working in the district than accountants. You may have depended on an assumption that accountants are more likely to be detailed persons. But even supposing 10 percent of teachers are detailed persons, in a large district odds that Mary is a teacher are still something on the order of 150-to-1. We all possess hidden assumptions; we just have to discover what they are.

Serving on a Board

As a business official, you may sit on any number of boards, ranging from a joint powers authority to a redevelopment district or from an educational cable TV commission to a state advisory council. Sitting on a board gives you an appreciation of the regular parliamentary finesse required each week by your own school board members. Use these tips to improve your personal parliamentary prowess.

1. Know your authorities; have them at hand.

Always know under what authority you are operating. Go to a meeting having read the statute, the bylaws or constitution. Also, know the authority for meeting procedures. Most groups operate on *Robert's Rules of Order*. But beware: there are variations. Some procedural books call them simply *Robert's Rules*. The real *Robert's Rules of Order* is more than 100 years old and was written by an army engineer who was embarrassed after running a chaotic church meeting. A copy of your board's rules should be on hand at each meeting as a reference.

2. Learn the rank and order of motions.
Motions can be grouped into categories, the most common type simply labeled as the "main motion." A main motion brings business before the meeting, but ranks lowest in the order of precedence. Other categories of motions include subsidiary motions (such as to postpone, amend, refer or table), privileged motions (such as to raise a point of privileges, recess or adjourn), and incidental motions (such as to raise a point of order, suspend the rules or make an inquiry).

3. Pre-think your motions; write out the long ones.
When you make a motion, go over it once in your mind before talking. Choose precise nouns and action verbs. Making a motion means action is going to result. The words will be recorded for all time in the official minutes. When issues get complicated, it is better to write out the motion and read it. We've all been in meetings where no one is sure what the motion says

or does. You will save embarrassment and time by preparing a clear statement.

4. As a chairperson, act impartially, but respect your rights.

The chair of a meeting is charged with running a fair meeting and respecting the rights of all to speak and be heard. Usually the chair of a board has the same voting rights and responsibilities as the other members of the group. However, the chair protects his or her impartiality by exercising voting rights only when his or her vote would affect the outcome. When the outcome is at stake, the chair can vote and directly change the result. The other alternative is to abstain, and if the vote results in a tie, the motion would fail for lack of affirmative votes.

5. Know when to leave.

Tired of meetings running late? A motion with high priority is a motion to fix the time to adjourn. The motion requires a second, and a majority to pass, but is not debatable. The same rules apply for a simple adjournment at the end of the meeting. Often, the chair makes the mistake of not asking for a second to adjourn. However, while the motion is pending it is acceptable for the chair or president to make announcements, to remind the group of business still needing attention, and to move to set the time for the next meeting, if not already determined. The vote can then be taken. The meeting is not officially closed until the chair says so. If an earlier motion is in effect setting the time and method for adjournment, no further motion is required.

6. Know why procedures are important.
Rules of order ensure that only one piece of business is conducted at a time, in a fair manner, with due consideration of minority viewpoints. If your group has adopted an official standard, it is important to be true to the standard. Ignoring the standards leaves your actions open for possible invalidation through appeals and legal challenges.

Enhancing Creativity

Do you need a solution to a problem in your district? If the old ways of doing things just aren't working, use a technique developed by Alex Osborn and Bob Eberle, experts in teaching creativity. Their techniques may help you find a new way to solve an old problem. Use the acronym SCAMPER to remember idea-spurring questions, as described in the book *Thinker Toys* by Michael Michalko. It is helpful to go through the entire range of questions before you decide one approach is the "right" solution. We will use the issue of school facilities as an example in this set of tips, but the same kinds of questions can be used for any school business problem.

1. Substitute.

Ask questions that allow a trial and error method of replacing one housing option with another. Sample questions to ask include: What can be substituted for student housing? Can we substitute populations? Can we substitute building types? Can we substitute schedules? Can we substitute grade levels? Can we substitute days in the schedule? Can we substitute staff? What other approaches could we use? Can rules be changed? Is there another procedure? Is there another location?

2. Combine.

Think about bringing together unrelated ideas, methods and services. Ask what housing can be combined? What programs can be combined? What kind of assortments of students can we make? What classes or grade levels could be merged? What properties could be packaged together? What districts and site services could be combined? How can we combine classrooms with some other facilities? Who could be brought together?

3. Adapt.

All new ideas are really offshoots of others or adaptations from prior experiences. Think how you can make adaptations to solve your housing problem. What else is this housing problem like? What is an analogy to this facility problem? What other industry could be copied? Can we adapt what colleges do? Can we take something from where parents go to work? What would this problem look like in a different context or environment? What districts can we emulate? What if we were to adapt this problem from the perspective of city government? How can we adapt current housing?

4. Modify and magnify.

Search for ways to add to, lengthen or multiply your existing housing options. Anything can be modified. Ask what can be made bigger? What can be extended? What can we add to? Can we go higher? Can we go lower? Can we add extra features? What about greater frequency? How about longer uses of buildings? How can we modify current facilities? How can we magnify the square footage we are currently using? Is there a new twist to staffing? Can we change a name and find a solution? Can we modify the process as well as the product?

5. Put to other uses.

Think about what else you can do with an existing solution. Ask if there are new ways to use buildings? Could we extend an existing plan? What else could be made? Can district office buildings be used differently? Can off-site locations help? Is there a new method of instructional delivery?

6. Eliminate.

Sometimes ideas come by subtracting. Omit the guns from a tank and you have a tractor. Ask yourself how could our population be smaller? Could we shrink the facility? Can rules be eliminated? What can we condense or compact? What would happen if we make miniature schools? What can we divide? What parts can be separated? Can we take away steps in the process? Can we streamline buildings?

7. Rearrange and reverse.

Creativity is really rearranging what we know in order to find new solutions. Move the pieces of your puzzle into different arrangements. Is there another pattern? How about a new grade configuration? Is there a better site layout? Is there a different attendance pattern? What if we changed the order in which we built? Can we transpose or group anything? What is the reverse of building new classrooms? What is the opposite of year-round school? What would happen if we reversed roles with the state, the developers or the city? What would happen if we turned a building a different direction? What would we see if we looked at the plans in a mirror?

Using Parent Notification Systems

A shooting, a chemical spill, an explosion – these are the kinds of emergencies that panic parents when their kids are at school and out of their direct control. If you face an emergency at one of your schools, your job will be harder if you have to spend time managing parents in addition to managing the crisis at hand. Parent management can be more difficult than the original emergency. The key to managing and reassuring parents of their children's safety is in preparation and communication. Use a robust emergency notification system in concert with your emergency plan to ensure you have reached all your constituents in a timely manner.

1. Avoid vendors with voice over Internet protocol systems.

The parent notification system you choose should bypass voice-over-Internet-protocol systems, integrate with a student database system, hold multiple types of contacts for any single student, and reach at least 1,000 people within five minutes. In choosing a system, think about the analogy of pouring water into a funnel. If you poor too much water in at a time, the water will overflow the edge of the funnel. The system you choose should be able to channel all your calls without "overflowing." A poorly engineered system leads to failed calls and angry parents.

2. Collect multiple addresses and phone numbers.

A notification system is only as good as the data that it stores. The best approach is one that has collected a home phone number, all cell phone numbers, and all email addresses for all parents and guardians related to one student. This includes both parents and step-parents who could have an interest in the safety of the student and who would have reason to contact the school in an emergency. Contracts should be ranked in order of importance. If a student suffers an illness, injury or personal emergency, the school will make a single contact in order of importance. If there is a schoolwide or neighborhood emergency, all contacts for all students will be reached using each phone number and address. This approach assures multiple coverage, meaning that a parent could get a text message, phone call and an email related to one schoolwide emergency. And that's good.

3. Make it easy for parents to update data.
Data change often, so parents should have the password-protected ability at any time to change their emergency contact information on-line. These online changes should integrate with the district's student database software, which, in turn, should integrate with district's emergency notification provider.

4. Maintain a library of emergency scripts.
Each school and the district should have emergency messages prewritten for a variety of emergency scenarios. Message contents should mirror the safety, protection, and evacuation protocols established in each school's emergency plan, but those messages will then be tweaked to cover the facts involving the emergency at hand. There's no sense in wasting 10 minutes trying to write a message from scratch when you are already multitasking on a real emergency. By having the body of your message ready, you can delegate changes to a subordinate and pay more attention to the emergency at hand.

5. Consider separate messages for staff and their families.

Have separate messages that notify the spouses and emergency contracts related to staff members. Review the emergency contract protocols with staff at a regular meeting, so they will know the sequence of communication events when an emergency happens. Announce to staff members that their emergency contacts are being notified, so that they can pay full attention to care for students. In an emergency it is easy for students to get lost or hurt if staff members are distracted trying to communicate their loved ones by email or a phone.

6. Craft message content with assurances and directions.

Message content should give assurances of student safety when it is a true statement. Contact information for students who are victims in an emergency can be suppressed from a mass notification, and parents of these students should be notified ahead of others. Second, messages should tell parents what to do. Third, messages should notify parents how and when the next message will come to them. Depend on your parent notification system to send out regular, timely and factual updates. Do not depend upon the news media, through whom the messages can be distorted and sensationalized.

7. Be careful releasing children when the emergency is over.

Finally, have a structured, verifiable method for releasing children to the right people when the time comes. Your mass notification, coupled with news media coverage of your emergency, could prompt estranged parents – or even strangers – to exploit the confusion to abduct children, leading to another emergency all of its own.

Resisting Accounting Temptations

R eports are due. You have an interest in making sure your budget, your financial statements and your state forms look good and match your projections. There are fewer gray areas in accounting than in most disciplines. Common sense, accounting standards and professional ethics require us as business officials to avoid the following temptations.

1. Booking revenue before it is earned.

It's clear: Don't book revenue before it is earned. For example, a contract for a grant will enable you to budget potential revenue, but the district must perform the work to get the money. Invoice, bill or make claims when the work is completed. You now have a receivable.

How many of your receivables can be collected? Book revenue when it is earned, not before.

2. Shifting expenses to a later reporting period.

An expense must be booked as an expense in the period in which the report was incurred. It doesn't matter whether your expense reports spike in one quarter; the object is to not have a sloping graphical curve. Controlling expenses over time is a management function before and while the expenses are incurred. Don't be tempted to delay recording information to produce nice reports. Don't let a pile of papers and a backlog of work delay your bookkeeping. Once the money goes, the accounting must be prompt and automatic; accounting is simply a truthful tape recorder of the ebb and flow of money.

3. Not disclosing district liabilities.

Have you done a districtwide search for liabilities? Do you have a master contracts file? Are your sites signing contracts without your knowledge? Have you calculated your potential liability for vacation payoffs? Have you disclosed your exposure for retiree health benefits? Is equipment obtained under a lease-purchase still existent, operating and logged for payout? Do you have uninspected facilities which could pose a liability for pay-backs to the state building program? Do you have a material difference in the book value of your investments? Find your liabilities and report them.

4. Shifting current income to a later period.

Don't be tempted to shift income to a later period to avoid the scrutiny of union negotiators. Don't hold income in a temporary reserve to avoid a proper reporting responsibility. If the money is in your bank, or if you are in receipt of a check, you are obliged to report the transaction in the proper period. It doesn't matter if you expected it after negotiations were done. Under reporting revenue is as bad as hiding expenses – a breach of professional ethics. Smoothing income usually results in unpleasant results down the road, especially in lean economic times.

5. Reporting phantom income.

This bad practice, when it sneaks through, usually finds its way through finance into budgets and reports to county and state officials, not necessarily into actual accounting records. Anticipation of money through a grant, a court settlement or a bond is not a sufficient basis upon which to testify to the state you have sufficient resources to meet your obligations. This egregious practice, while rare, has been the downfall of several districts, forcing them to turn to the state for loans and outside trustees.

6. Shifting future expenses to a current or earlier period.

Districts anticipating a large ending balance or unexpected income may be tempted to shift future expenses into the last period of a fiscal year or an earlier period. Don't do it. Buying a year's worth of postage on June 29 will not give management or the board a clear picture of the district's financial status. Accounting is designed to record and give clear pictures. Don't solicit vendors for early invoices or pay for goods and services not received. Legitimately expensed advances and deposits are duly noted as prepayments.

Building Budget Documents

B ased on the standards for a meritorious budget, as composed by the Association of School Business Officials International, these tips will help you assemble the ingredients for an excellent school budget document.

1. Start with a dynamic introductory section.

Use an executive summary that can be lifted independently out of your larger document. Make sure it clearly summarizes all funds, compares the budget year to the past and your prediction of the future, includes simple and easily understandable charts and graphs, details any significant policy changes, and explains how resources are allocated to achieve your goals and objectives. The introductory section should be preceded by a table of contents for the entire document and followed with a listing of the board and first-level staff with phone numbers and contact information.

2. Create a comprehensive organizational section.
Include in this section the district's mission, goals and objectives, an organizational chart, an overview of the budget development process and the process of budget administration and management. Also include a discussion of budget and financial policies, state rules and regulations guiding the budget process and any local policy requirements affecting the budget.

3. Provide solid explanations in the financial section.
Explain the financial structure of the district by fund and by the classification of revenues and expenditures. Present revenues by source and expenditures by function and object. Also, consider presentations by program, location and administrative unit. Use a pyramid approach, which begins with a summary of all funds and then presents individual funds, followed by detail. Make sure to include fund balances, revenues, and expenditures for the current (prior) year and the budget year, both at the same level of detail. Explain the basis for budgeting in each fund. Describe underlying assumptions for revenue, the funding structure, and funding trends. List capital expenditures and projects

for the year. Describe how capital improvements will affect current and future operating budgets. Include information on current debt obligations, and debit-level to debt-limit ratios.

4. Build community understanding with an informational section.

Place a multi-year summary comparison of revenues and expenditures in this section. Although difficult to compile in some states, also include a multiyear budget forecast, with appropriate caveats. Also publish a student enrollment history, enrollment forecasting methodology, assessed value of property taxed for local bonds, bond amortization schedules, an explanation of revenue limit calculations, and any performance measures used in the district. Such measures could include test scores, satisfaction surveys, dropout rates, performance audit findings or written descriptions of how goals and objectives were attained. Include a glossary of terms.

Avoiding Grant Writing Pitfalls

Whether you are writing a grant or hiring someone else to write a grant for you, it is essential that you understand the basics underlying grant writing. Among the most frequent reasons why grants are denied include:

1. Not understanding that the funder has an agenda. Even free money is not free. A corporation or foundation giving grants has an agenda, a purpose it wants fulfilled. Your activities have to enhance the grantor's objectives, while accomplishing yours at the same time. If you spend too much time selling screeners on your objectives, you are likely to be turned down.

2. Not following directions or program guidelines.

It's simple. The donors have a format that makes screening applications work for the system they have established. Violate the directions and your grant application is guaranteed to be tossed. There are plenty of other people who have followed the directions, so why should they pay attention to your nonconformist application?

3. Using vague generalizations and rambling thought.

To avoid generalizations, practice this procedure: Read your narrative. Does each sentence let you create a specific visual picture of what you want to happen? Use words – both nouns and verbs – that help people create a mental picture. Instead of saying students, describe the type of students, such as "teenage girls," or "5-year-olds with a passion for reading."

4. Making unsubstantiated claims.

Are you promising the world without building any foundation for trust? Do you claim that your program has already had its desired effect? Then spell out what evaluation procedure brought you to this conclusion. The more you document and substantiate, the more likely you are to build trust for someone to give you money.

5. Proposing an unrealistic budget.

Are you asking for too much? Could you even possibly organize your program and spend the money requested in the time you have allotted? Have you proposed a match with money over which you have no control? The more realism you bring to your budget proposal, the more likelihood screeners will move your application forward.

6. Overusing a boilerplate grant proposal.

Screeners can detect a cut-and-paste job from the outside of the envelope, figuratively speaking. If you have just dusted off language from another grant proposal, your application is likely to fall to the bottom of the donor's stack. The funders are interested in people who have put some thought into an idea. After all, it is their money they are giving away. If you have not paid them the attention they deserve, you are in the same category as a person begging for money at the exit of a freeway.

Choosing a Lobbyist

A day will come when you need a lobbyist, either to influence a piece of legislation or to promote your interests in front of a state agency. Contracting or hiring a great advocate requires you to study firms and personalities in advance of your decision. Use these tips when assessing potential firms and candidates, developing your RFPs and conducting your interviews.

1. Find someone who plays your game.

Tobacco or oil lobbyists may have plenty of clout with legislators, but when it comes to explaining the impact of legislation on student achievement, bell schedules or revenue limit deficits, they are likely to fall on their face. Choose a lobbyist who knows your subject. When necessary, choose a specialist – for example, one who focuses solely on the facilities issue. Based on the experience of other districts, out-of-their-field advocates can't deliver as effectively as those who know education inside and out.

2. Ask questions that get at sources and contacts.

You may be surprised to learn that some lobbyists live off the information provided by other lobbyists in meetings and hearings. Sharing is important in the education community, but some lobbyists do not even read basic source materials such as budget books and Legislative Analyst reports. Find a lobbyist who does extensive reading, who reviews the details in the actual bills. Find a lobbyist who has contacts to get information before it is in print.

3. Protect "on task" time.

Consider how to protect your investment in a lobbyist. You want assurances that a lobbyist is actually spending time on your issue, not just strolling the hall talking to friends. Your protection can come in the form of oral or written reports, listings of contacts made, testimony provided and copies of letters written. Build in a reporting mechanism that assures you that your advocate is busy on your issue.

4. Plan for results, but accept no promises.

Lobbyists who promise they can get you something are breaking the law. No one is allowed to promise or guarantee that he or she can influence a decision, law or rule to be enacted one way or another. However, a qualified lobbyist would plan for results. Choose a lobbyist who can craft a plan: "We need these votes." "These people must be contacted in the district." "Send letters from these individuals." "Be prepared to compromise on this detail." "Testify on these points." Expect a plan; don't let a lobbyist fly by the seat of his or her pants on your issue. Though there are times lobbyists go by instinct, there is no substitute for a detailed written strategy.

5. Choose credibility over credentials.

If you find a lobbyist with great credentials, check on credibility, as well. Your lobbyist represents you. You don't want your district's name associated with representatives who lie, don't deliver on promises, violate rules, bad talk your district behind your back or treat people poorly. Credibility also means avoiding conflict of interest. A lobbyist should not take your money if he or she already has a client with a competing interest. Check on credibility by checking references and contacting legislators and legislative staff about your candidate's reputation. Also, request a comprehensive listing of the lobbyist's current and recent clients.

6. Opt for multiple modes of influence.

Lawmaking is so complex today, no one style of lobbying is best suited for any one issue. For example, it may not be enough that your potential lobbyist is a former capital staffer with contacts to committee chairs. You may need a multifaceted firm or individual who also knows media, one who knows grassroots organizing techniques, one who regularly makes campaign contributions, one who can quickly develop policy compromises or creative approaches, one who can build alliances among associations and special-interest groups, one who can testify well and one who can get along with the gatekeepers who protect members of the state Legislature. In other words, big money and the good ol' boys alone do not get the results they used to. Advocacy is now a more sophisticated blend of politics, art and science.

Managing Your Time

In today's fast-paced environment, everyone feels pressed for time. The demands placed on individuals today are greater than ever. It is beneficial to periodically review your use of time, and in particular determine whether you can streamline your activities. Use these tips to get a handle on your time management skills and leave more time for yourself.

1. Audit your time.

At least once a year, document how you spend your waking hours for an entire typical week. Analyze your time using this newly created document, and then make adjustments for yourself and your work.

2. Schedule goal-oriented activity.

Always schedule around a major goal, event or important task. Schedule the other mundane and routine items around the task necessary to reach the goal. Every workday should have a goal-oriented focus. You and your administrative assistant should plan your schedule weekly, and then review each day one day in advance.

3. Record your interruptions.

The people who are closest to you are probably the people who interrupt the most. Keep a log of interruptions and study them for patterns. Schedule regular blocks of time with people who work with you on a daily basis. When you get a formidable interruption, use the stand-up technique. Don't sit down. People will get to the point quickly and be on their way.

4. Conquer unpleasant tasks.

Difficult or unpleasant tasks are easily neglected. Procrastinating on these items will cost you more time in the end. The best way to handle the ugly jobs is to break them into segments. Then set aside priority time to work each component task. Reward yourself when the job is completed.

5. Make decisions quickly.

You will bottleneck work for yourself and your office

if you put off making decisions. The two main enemies of quick decision making are lack of information and fear. First, foster an environment in your office where it is OK to make mistakes as long as you learn and move forward. Second, establish a mechanism to get full information on an issue before it reaches your desk.

6. Establish real deadlines.

Work always expands to fill the time allotted to it. Therefore, establish real deadlines that others keep you accountable to meet. Sometimes the extra polish you put on a job takes you beyond a reasonable allocation of your time. You are needed elsewhere. Do an excellent job. Then stop and go on to the next task.

7. Know how to end.

Meetings are the number one consumer of an administrator's time. It is important to define, first of all, the goal of a meeting. Set the entire focus on meeting the goal. Don't stray to side topics. When discussion is nearly complete, summarize the meeting. Ask if any final points need to be made. Then, announce the action, make assignments or delineate necessary follow-up steps.

Improving Warehouse Safety

The operation of district warehouses is often delegated to directors of purchasing or general services, but safety is everyone's concern. Take note of these tips when reviewing the safety of your warehouse.

1. Practice control.

That means take precautions over what is purchased, stored and transported in and out of the warehouse. To practice reasonable control, for example, you must read material safety data sheets, deliberately purchase less toxic supplies, store chemical families together, rotate stock, develop policies regarding the juxtaposition of supplies, and monitor quantities.

2. Practice containment.

Once something is in your warehouse, take care to ensure the safety of the materials. For example, take earthquake precautions, chain down tanks, use proper storage containers, and – with training – eliminate human errors that lead to spills, falls and injury.

3. Practice effective clean up.

One of the most common warehouse mishaps is an accidental spill, and if the spill involves chemicals, you have to be ready. Always be prepared for clean-up. Have a spill control pillow on hand. Know the location of sewers and drains to divert runoffs to a safe area. Post a procedure for spills, falls and injuries that exceed the ability of your staff to handle. Know the phone number of the county environmental health office and the Environmental Protection Agency before there is a problem.

4. Practice regular staff training and retraining.

When it comes to safety, training should never stop. Pay special attention to fork lift training, a big potential for problems. Test and certify fork lift operators. Study hazardous materials management. Inform employees about proper and safe dress for the warehouse. Explain and demonstrate lifting procedures. Monitor injury claims and make changes to avoid future problems.

5. Practice good housekeeping.

We take warehouses for granted, but they need maintenance. Treat floors with a non-combustible sealer. Ensure good lighting, heat and ventilation. Ask your warehouse employees about their comfort. Keep floors clear of pallets, containers and debris. Establish policies for the immediate removal and recycling of packaging materials. Inspect shelving frequently. Eliminate dust and moisture that can ruin goods.

6. Practice fire prevention.

Establish a regular fire prevention walk-through routine and check-off system. Practice evacuations. Keep driveways and lanes clear for fire vehicles at all times. Post "no smoking" signs and move outside smoking areas away from the warehouse. Design and maintain storage with firefighting in mind.

7. Practice solid security.

Have a single master key and keep the spare in the district vault. Limit unauthorized access. Set the supervisor's work station in a spot for clear visibility to entry and exit points. Monitor the activities of delivery drivers. Keep your warehouse vandal proof. Construct a security cage for small high-value items. Inventory regularly.

Moving Your Analog Mind to the Digital Age

D o you constantly get the feeling that you are about to lose track of developments in technology? Today it's not enough to keep on top of the disciplines associated with your job; regardless of your position and your industry, it is to your greatest benefit to learn about new technological trends as well. Why? Not only could you be doing your job faster with more advanced equipment, but you also don't want to give the impression to your customers that you are satisfied with the status quo. Plus, emerging technology can be exciting.

1. Try a new software package or app for an actual district project that needs completion.
You can study and take classes all you want, but jumping

in and using a new product is the best way to learn a
new category of software or mobile applications, be
it presentation software, a database or a publishing
program. Branch out and try using a product that is not
mainstream. The methodology of different software
engineers may spark new ideas for you.

2. Survey old routines and automate.

Still doing things the old fashioned way? Scan your
department for routines that could be automated with
new technology. You may not know what the new
technology is, but if you are passing a lot of papers
across desks or managing multiple databases, there is
probably a new technology to handle it. For example,
consider imaging for personnel records, eCommerce for
purchasing, optical character recognition for free lunch
applications, and mapping programs for bus routes.

3. Read *The Wall Street Journal.*

Probably the best all-around publication to keep
busy business leaders up to speed on technology, the
Journal has a regular technology section online. It
also has a personal technology column. Big company
advertisements announce leading edge advancements
in technology – ideas you would have never dreamed
of. Regular articles and white papers alert you to new
products. For example, readers of the *Journal* recently

learned that supercookies are a threat to computer security, being able to able to reclaim deleted browsing histories, and that microwave radar may soon be ready for blind-spot detection around school buses.

4. Ask the "gadgets" and "gizmos" question.
When you are out and about with acquaintances, talking at parties, watching kids' baseball games, or playing golf, ask people about what new apps, gadgets, gizmos and other new technology they are using in their jobs. Hopefully, they will not reveal any company secrets and have to kill you, but they may be able to share some unique insights in an industry outside of education. Take it one step further and see if any of their applications could be used in your district.

5. Get your nose into a computer magazine.
If you can't stomach subscribing to another publication, buy a computer magazine at the grocery store now and then. The personal computer, the smart phone, and the Internet will continue to be cornerstones of new developments in technology. Following developments on those three fronts alone will keep you miles ahead of your competition in the digital age. Scan your magazine for new developments in software. Emerging companies often debut new ideas for niche software applications in these pages.

6. Watch kids.

Watch what kids are buying and playing with. They are on the leading edge and are not afraid to be early adapters. Toys are often dumbed down versions of technology that have a higher purpose. Teenagers know that Pandora and Spotify are emerging ways to listen to music. What's the impact on how you purchase recordings for your schools? Kids are playing games with each other over the Internet. Mobile learning on phones and tablets will soon follow.

Improving Internal Controls

No organization – large or small – can ignore internal accounting controls. It's a fundamental fiduciary responsibility, so fundamental it's often taken for granted. Now is the time to take a second look.

1. Set a positive tone for review before there is a problem.

Explain to your team that now is the time to look at internal controls – before there is trouble. Make the review a positive experience without fear and suspicion. Set aside a dedicated time for discussion without any other business. Involving the staff will point you to vulnerabilities you did not know existed.

2. Brainstorm weak control points.

Assemble members of your team together and ask the questions, "If someone wanted to steal from the district, what would be the easiest way for them to do that without getting caught? What are the weakest links in our internal controls?" Team members should be able to contribute to the discussion without fear that they will be reprimanded for pointing out weaknesses in their own departments.

3. Physically survey locations where cash is collected.

After you have brainstormed weak control points, make some personal visits. While you are physically at a location, ask yourself, "Are procedures in place to prevent or detect loss of collections? Are the collections deposited regularly? Prior to deposit, are these collections maintained in a safe place? Are collections reconciled?"

4. Inventory your property.

Although the task is daunting, make sure you regularly inventory district equipment. Small tools, electronic equipment and furniture can easily float among school campuses, departments and offices. Whose is it when it moves? Ask managers to be accountable for equipment under their supervision. Spell out how and when equipment can move.

5. Institute personnel controls.

Make sure employees are taking vacation. Banks, for example, require mandatory vacations, thwarting the possibility that employees can perpetuate fraud while they are absent. Are family members who work for the same district segregated sufficiently to prevent collusion? Are background checks made before employees are hired?

6. Secure your high tech devices.

Not everybody is at the same level of knowledge with regard to technology. Are your systems secure to keep out hackers or employees with a high degree of sophistication in technology? Do your managers know what signs and behaviors to watch out for? Are employees' screens easily monitored? Are modems to the outside secure from employees working at home? Are passwords changed regularly? Are sufficient controls in place for IT employees who maintain your computers? Are you vulnerable if an IT staff member terminates employment?

7. Communicate appropriate values and ethics to all employees.

To prevent problems and develop a culture of trust, develop values statements and statements of ethics for all employees. Communicate these values to employees, not just upon being hired, but at periodic unexpected intervals. These kinds of communications help eliminate gray areas and give employees an additional reason to do the right thing.

Interpreting Survey Results

Polls can be important measures of public opinion. They can also be falsely used to make a case for a cause. Some people swear by survey research; others don't believe any survey statistic. Who is right? While surveys can give you useful information about where the public stands on pertinent issues, you must look closely at the nature of both the survey instrument and the individual questions before giving them credence.

1. Analyze the questions.

Before taking poll results as gospel, analyze the questions. Your interpretation may be completely different from the person interviewed. One word can make a difference in a response. If you are working on a poll, realize that the way interviewers inflect words can affect the response. It is best to have disinterested persons asking the questions.

2. Look at the numbers and the margin of error.

The survey sample must be of sufficient size to be representative. A survey's margin of error depends on the number of people surveyed compared with the total number of people in the relevant population. A survey of 500 will be more prone to error than one of 2,000. However, sample sizes over 2,000 usually have little statistical change. Your polling firm should calculate the margin of error. Before making a decision based on polls, factor in the error against your position. When analyzing the results of another organization's poll, make sure the number of respondents and margin of error is included in the description of the survey. Companies and newspapers often omit these important numbers.

3. Trends are more important than a single poll.

The trend of polls, especially over a recent period, is more reflective of reality than one poll. If a new poll falls within trend lines, then you can depend on the pattern and positions reflected more than one single poll. If your poll falls outside trend lines, beware. There could be bias in questioning, respondents may be lying, or your questions may be bad. In addition, a recent event may temporarily influence respondents' opinions, so pay attention to surrounding factors.

4. Prepare to poll more than once.

Situations change. People's opinions change. Media events affect perceptions. Campaigns sway undecided voters. If all your work is based on an early poll, you may be headed in the wrong direction. Poll again close to decision points if you want absolute accuracy.

5. Beware of generalizing from cross-tabulated populations.

Some poll reports or firms focus on small groups in the population that comprise a tiny proportion of the total sample. For example, a sample of 1,000 voters may contain just 15 special education parents. It would be unwise to believe that those 15 could accurately reflect the views of all special education parents.

6. Examine the track record of the group or polling firm.

When reading outside polls, always find out who paid for the poll. Read the poll with that bias. Better yet, procure a copy of the actual questions. Some firms -- sometimes the low cost bidders -- have a limited track record in carrying out surveys. Always check on methodology, the experience of the field force and interviewers, and the quality of the analysis. Analysis may be more important than poll results themselves.

7. Don't generalize from open-ended questions.

Occasionally polls, surveys or evaluations will ask open ended questions that give a respondent an opportunity to discuss likes or dislikes, opine about an issue or raise topics of interest. Don't generalize from these responses. Although they make interesting reading, these responses are not representative of an entire population. Many administrators act to change a system based on the concern of a population of one person.

8. Make sure your staff shares your perception of risk.

Once you have determined a degree of risk associated with a course of action, you should share your assessment with your staff and others in your organization. Those charged with the implementation of a decision can act in a way that is either too conservative or too liberal. The conservative staff member may forfeit opportunities and the liberal employee may expose you to failure. Help others to understand how you perceive the risks, so they can chart the course you have set.

Extending the Life of Roofs

D rip. Drip. Drip. Do you have an effective system for maintaining school roofing? The life of a roof can be extended, if we pay attention and put systems in place for regular treatment of existing construction and routine maintenance. How do these seven tips compare to your existing habits to reduce the life cycle costs of your roofs?

1. Build a roof file.

Prepare a file for each roof under your supervision. File contents should describe roof materials, construction type and contractors. Include warranties, as well as a photograph and description of the roof in its baseline condition. Include a drawing with dimensions and slopes. Keep a log of complaints and work orders. Start the file the day your district accepts a building. For old buildings, start today.

2. Create a log and control access.
Roofs should be accessible only to authorized personnel. Traffic causes damage. Post signs. If needed, create barriers to keep students off. Once controls are in place, create an access log, maintained by a building administrator or school secretary. Persons accessing the roof must sign in and out. Hold anyone with access accountable for roof damage.

3. Establish regular inspection dates.
Using your file, drawings and photographs, inspect the roof at least annually. Make condition comparisons. Take new photographs. Follow an inspection checklist and take care to peruse flashing around pipes, drains and expansion joints. Write on copies of your drawings, noting problems found during your inspection – ponding water, broken tiles, torn membranes, etc. Check attic spaces and ceilings. Talk to people who work inside. They will alert you to inconspicuous problems. Compare results to the file's baseline data.

4. Do double duty.
While your crews are on the roof for the inspection, have them carry a small broom and trash bag. Clear away

debris, PE equipment, leaves and other foreign materials. This saves manpower and minimizes roof traffic. It may also prevent drains from clogging.

5. Triage the results.

Use your reports to determine the severity of problems and method of repair. Some problems will generate immediate work orders to prevent further damage. Other work may be added to your major maintenance schedule or roof work plan. Every problem must be scheduled for repair. Detail the disposition of all problems in the roof file. No damage should go unrepaired.

6. Establish a reporting system.

Make it clear to teachers and site personnel that all leaks and roofing problems are to be reported. In some cases, buildings leak so often that people assume someone already knows. Include leak reports in the roof file. Report back to sites what your plan is for repair, even if it is part of a long-range major maintenance schedule.

7. Get smart about leaks.

Water is sneaky. It comes from places you would least expect. It can travel great distances. Never assume a leak is coming from directly above. Always remove ceiling tiles to avoid further damage. Follow the source of the moisture. Document the problem in the file. Take pictures. Verify whether repairs fall under warranties. A rainy-day repair is usually a stop-gap repair. Return and fix it right. Hire professional roofers when necessary.

Using Commas Correctly

Over at the high school, English teachers are explaining the common 14 justifiable reasons to use a comma in writing. Here at the business office, we too often stick a comma in our prose because we think it makes the writing sound good when read aloud, not because we have a good reason. Here are six of the comma rules broken most often in our business writing.

1. Separate items in series.

Use the comma to separate items in a series not completely linked by one of the following conjunctions: *and, or, not, yet, but, so, for*. Here's an example of the correct way to use commas: "I am buying paper, computers and custodial supplies." Here is an example of incorrect usage: "Transcripts, and report cards were high priorities for data processing." In the first example no comma is necessary because the conjunction *and* joins computers and custodial supplies. The most popular media omit the comma in this example. This is illustrative of the so-called "Harvard comma" controversy. Uppity book publishers will include the comma in this instance, even though it technically violates the first rule.

2. Set off long introductory phrases.

It is correct to use a comma after an introductory prepositional phrase containing five or more words. If the phrase contains fewer than five words, do not use the comma. Here is a correct example: "In the middle of negotiations with teachers, our administrators received a call from the classified unit announcing it would sign off on the tentative agreement." Here is an example of incorrect punctuation: "In Buena Park, the boundaries are well defined."

3. Use the word *not* as a clue for contrasting expressions.

Commas set off contrasting expressions introduced by the word *not*. For example, it is correct to write, "The interim report is due Monday, not Friday." Notice that the word *and* is usually unnecessary in these situations.

Also notice that contrasting expressions sometimes need to be set off on both sides, as in this example: "Enrollment accounting, not attendance accounting, is the crux of the debate."

4. Join independent clauses with a comma, if they are also joined with a conjunction.

First let's define an independent clause. If the expression or phrase can be a sentence all by itself, it is an independent clause. If you link the clauses with one of the following words *and*, *or*, *not, yet, but, so,* and *for,* then use a comma, as in the following example: "You sign the checks, and I will prepare the registers." Be cautious: if you don't use one of those conjunctive words, you will need to use a semicolon, and not a comma. Here's an example: "The account is totally encumbered; I will call and ask for a budget transfer form." Now that you are an expert, what is wrong with the following sentence? "The position is vacant and you are welcome to apply." You're right. It needs a comma after the word "vacant."

5. A comma is a friend when you rename a friend.

In grammatical terms we are talking about "appositives." An appositive is a name, term or expression that renames an immediately preceding noun or pronoun. When you use an appositive, set the word or phrase off with commas. This rule is more easily understood if you look at an example: "Tom Torlakson, California's state superintendent of public instruction, held a press conference in our district." The words "California's state superintendent of public instruction" rename "Torlakson." Set off the renamed words on both sides with commas. Another correct example is: "San Diego, America's finest city, saw rain five out of the last seven days of summer."

6. Yes, commas with *yes* and *no*, not periods.
Your boss leaves you a sticky note, asking if you are attending the meeting. Invoke the following rule: Use commas to set off words like *yes* and *no* when used as responses. For example, "Yes, the meeting is still on." Or in the negative, the correct written response would be: "No, I understand they are not signing up." Now determine whether the following usage is correct or incorrect: "Yes. We're going."

Giving a 5-Minute Presentation

If your Board of Education's agenda is lengthy, members probably want to move along quickly. Use these tips to deliver an effective presentation in just five minutes and still get your point across. Even if you are allotted a longer time slot, prepare for a short presentation. You will often need it.

1. Start with the recommendation first. Use 30 seconds or less.

Begin by flat out stating your recommendation. This is ultimately what you are getting to anyway. Think like news writers. The most important information is always given first. There is no sense hiding it or postponing it for later. Members have your written background information anyway. If the recommendation is shocking or controversial, admit such; then conclude your recommendation with the words, "I'll explain why it's the best and most reasonable approach, but first, here's some background."

2. Give the "what" and "why" review. Use 60 seconds or less.

State why this issue is before the board. How did it become an issue? Who are the players? Where are the land mines? Before your meeting, make one-sentence summaries of all the issues. Use these sentences as your notes. Avoid temptations to directly read the notes or fill in additional details. If you did your work ahead of time, your one-sentence summaries will tell the story. As you speak, refer board members to the appropriate detail in the written handouts, especially if they want more information. Make it their responsibility to have read their material before the meeting.

3. Explain the details of the recommendation. Use 60 seconds or less.

It is not necessary to restate your recommendation verbatim. This is the time to explain how the suggested course of action will work. Technical details go here. Explain any ramification and potential political fallout. Advise them on how these problems can be overcome.

Use one-sentence bullet points as notes. Once again, you can refer trustees to their written materials.

4. Outline the benefits of the suggested approach. Use 60 seconds or less.

Come right out with the words, "If you adopt the recommendation, we can expect . . ." Then list what you predict will go right. When possible, always promote the benefits of efficiency, savings of public money and enhancements for student achievement. Using quantitative data to support your claims will increase credibility. This is the time to remind the board of any follow-up evaluation you plan. Don't get syrupy. State your assessment of the benefits succinctly and candidly.

5. Think of a quick story or quote. Use 30 seconds.

Now you've been speaking for more than three minutes. Pull out a quick anecdote or quotation to transition yourself for the close. It can be light or funny, but doesn't have to be (funny stories from amateurs usually fail). But the story has to be about people and life. It can be a compliment to a staff member or real-life people-oriented details of how you deliberated on this decision. Mention names, places, students, schools, feelings and moods. This reminds decision-makers that we are in the people business, ultimately serving students.

6. Close by asking for action to get the benefits.
Use 60 seconds or less.

There should be no doubt about what trustees must do when you finish speaking. Do you need one motion or two? Ask for a unanimous vote. Reiterate the timeline. Restate the recommendation in broad terms, advising the board that if it adopts the recommendation it will see benefits of X, Y and Z. Thank the board members for their time, then offer to take any questions. Remember that follow-up questions are further opportunities for you to explain the positive benefits of your approach.

7. Know your speaking fundamentals.

Your presentation will be better and proceed more quickly if you look at each board member in the eyes in rotation. Look at a board member on the right, then left, then middle. Repeat left, right, then middle. Practice throwing out the *ums* and the *you knows*. Speak faster than normal conversation, but slower than oral readers – about 150 words per minute. A double-spaced page of typewritten text takes about 90 seconds to deliver, but don't read. And don't memorize. Practice the art of almost memorizing.

Performing Exit Interviews

Employees often have the most comprehensive knowledge about their jobs. When an employee leaves for greener pastures, it is your responsibility to tap into as much information as possible from that employee, prior to his or her departure. Not only can you get a better picture of the individual position's responsibilities, but you may also find valuable insights into what does and does not work in a department as a whole. Consider the following tips for conducting successful exit interviews.

1. Establish an exit interview policy and practice with employees.
It is easy to let the practice of conducting exit interviews fall through the cracks, because the people who have

the information are on their way out the door. There is little pressure for exiting employees to be accountable. If you do not currently conduct exit interviews with employees who are leaving, start the practice. If you do have an exit interview process, implement a policy to ensure the interviews and surveys are done promptly and efficiently. This is important information that will serve you for a long time.

2. Practice the utmost in integrity.

To get good information, the people leaving must feel comfortable in being honest with you. How honest and open they are about their feelings will depend on how you use and share the information. Your plans on how to use the information you gather should be shared with the employee who is leaving. Establish a reputation that can be trusted. Use the information only exactly as you said you would. If you change polices on how you use the feedback from terminated employees, the information gathered under an old policy should not be used subsequently in a way that would violate their trust.

3. Define your purpose for interviews.

It is surprising how many districts collect exit information because of tradition, not because they have a purpose in mind. Do you want to use the information to retard employee turnover? Do you want it for recruitment? Do you want to compare salaries and benefits? Do you want a pulse on employee morale? Whatever your purpose, you must then use these goals to formulate the interview or survey questions. Make sure your all questions asked are pertinent. In addition, institute a process to get the information out of a folder and into the hands of the people who must make changes. Too many exit surveys are now sitting in file folders with no purpose.

4. Define a role for various departments and divisions.

If your exit survey points out problems – for example, work overload, lack of technology or lack of challenging work – the department affected must be involved in a constructive and non-threatening way. Too often, the information collected from exit surveys or interviews does not find its way back to the department or division where the employee worked. The most powerful change is going to be back at the department or division level. Often, administrators and supervisors will have solutions if they know a problem exists.

5. Interview or survey employees who transfer.

Consider using an exit survey for employees who leave one department for another. Even if the employee is leaving for reasons of career advancement, his or her insight may be useful for your defined purposes. Since these employees generally like working for the district, they may have an added incentive of providing information that will improve overall operations or personnel practices.

6. When necessary, aggregate data.
If you or exiting employees are concerned about retribution, stigmas, bad references or other negative effects emanating from an honest exit interview, consider aggregating data from multiple employees and keeping names hidden. This is especially useful where there are many employees working in a school or division. If departments are smaller, consider issuing reports less frequently.

7. Consider using disinterested interviewers.
A department head may conduct his own survey or interview of a departing employee for his or her own edification. However, in conducting interviews face-to-face, a disinterested party will get better information from the exiting employees. Likewise, a survey turned into the personnel department will be more candid than one delivered to a soon-to-be former boss.

Bidding Outside Printing Jobs

If you have a district print shop, you may still choose to outsource complicated printing jobs, especially for books and four-color work. Use your own print shop as a resource for outsourcing and follow these tips.

1. Beware that paper is the No. 1 way bids are skewed.

Extra costs and profits can be buried in paper. When bidding printing, specify an exact manufacturer, grade, weight, texture and color of paper. Have the paper costs itemized. Ask for an option to use a house paper. This gives you a second price. Being specific means all printers will have to bid the same paper. The differences in paper price will force out the spread in actual printing costs. Once you know the actual printing costs, only then can you legitimately accept a printer's house paper to get an even better price with the low-cost printer.

2. Ask for increments of 1,000.

Another way to compare for printing is to ask for an option for additional lots of, say, 1,000 copies printed on a specific paper. Compare the lot price among printers.

3. Ask for blue lines and color keys.

If you want to make sure your final product is free of errors, build in a request for a blue line proof and a color key into your bid. A blue line is monotone mock-up of how your job will be assembled. It is created from the actual computer files used to make the plates. Color keys show you how and where colors of your job will appear when printed. Once you get these proofs, check for pagination, correctly aligned copy and properly placed color. This is the worst (most expensive) point to make changes in words or copy.

4. Agree on charges for alterations.

Agree on what the alteration charges will be ahead of time. Printers usually do not like to advertise these costs. They make lots of money on them. Alteration charges increase at each step of the printing process. Alterations consist of changes that you choose to make from your original submission of the job. Inadequate preparation or carelessly proofed copy can cost you more than you'd ever dream. If you know the costs going in, you can decide if making the change is worth the cost.

5. Watch out for overs and unders.

If you order 10,000 copies of a job, typical printing conventions say that delivery of 10 percent fewer or more than 10,000 is acceptable. You will be expected to pay for 10 percent more or less, as they are delivered. This mechanism is how the printer compensates for spoilage during printing. If you need exactly 10,000, and no less, the percentage of tolerance must be doubled. Therefore, be prepared to pay for 20 percent more copies than you actually need.

6. Separate out type and design costs at an hourly rate.

If your job is not camera ready or ready on disk, you may have typesetting and design charges. Agree on an hourly rate with a cap. Art is subjective; agree on guidelines. Typesetting errors made by the printer are the printer's responsibility and should be corrected at no cost. Any changes to your copy will cost you at the hourly rate or an alteration charge. Hourly rates are usually billed at minimum quarter-hour blocks.

7. Count the copies you receive.

It is not unusual that actual copies you receive fail to match copies billed on an invoice. It is more tedious to count brochures than to count books; however, you should plan on counting any item, no matter how tedious the process. Weighing product is the fastest method. Alternatively, check boxes for any counts listed. Test and sample boxes. Check for packing or wadded papers that may put some boxes short. Count out about 200 brochures. Keep a printer's paper gauge in the receiving warehouse to measure the thickness of a lot you've chosen to count. Use the gauge to count the rest of the box, then make an estimation based on your sampling.

Testifying in Court

As a business official, you may someday be called upon to testify in court or in a deposition. Review these tips for help as you become involved in litigation that requires your testimony.

1. Leave time to adequately prepare before your testimony.

This may require weeks or months of forethought and review, depending on the case. Review any documents you have that relate to the case. Be aware of others who may testify. Keep appointments with your attorneys. Practice answering questions. Even consider using an audio or video tape to review and assess how you sound answering questions.

2. Do not only tell the truth, think the truth.

It's a given that you should tell the absolute truth in your testimony. However, you should take extra care to think about the truth as well and ingrain the truth in your memory. Attorneys may take measures to ask questions in an unusual way that elicits a response the attorney wants, but may not be absolutely true in your mind or may give the wrong impression. Thinking the truth keeps you on track and thwarts an attorney from eliciting a casual comment from you that is more the attorney's thinking than yours.

3. Do not testify beyond the questions.

Don't volunteer more information than you have to. It is a natural tendency, especially of helpful business officials, to want to explain your answers as you would in normal conversation. Answer the exact question put to you, even if it only requires a yes or no answer. It is not your job to educate the attorney about school finance or school construction. Let your attorney work for you. Signs that you should be careful about giving too much information include objections from your own attorney, questions that are broad and open-ended, questions asked repeatedly, and questions including the words *always* and *never*.

4. Stay emotionally cool.

Attorneys can rattle you with their questions and can elicit an emotional response that may serve their purposes later. Even if big money is on the line, you should attempt to focus simply on the question and tell the truth. If you get angry, you use extra energy and can become nervous. You may become defensive and lose focus on the questions. If you feel provoked, channel the feelings away from the individual asking the questions and use them to help you answer questions more effectively.

5. Don't strategize or become defensive on the stand.

Trust your attorney to think about the dynamics of the trial or the deposition. Don't fashion your answers based on whether you think your testimony will move the case one way or another. Don't answer in an attempt to second guess what an attorney wants. Instead, truthfully answer the questions. Realize that oddly phrased questions are sometimes necessary to test your credibility, not to put you on trial.

6. Follow up after the testimony.

Anything you testify to can be brought up later in court or in settlement conferences. After a deposition, review the transcript for transcription mistakes before you sign. Attorneys will look for inaccurate or inconsistent statements in the transcript. Know what you said because your words will be indexed and cross referenced. Don't make comments on your testimony to others after the fact. These words, too, can come back to haunt you.

Working with the Media

Undoubtedly, you will be interviewed at some point by the news media about an issue related to school business. Every encounter with the media is your opportunity to get a message across. Media relations are key to public relations.

1. It's your interview; you set the agenda.
When a reporter interviews you, don't talk around questions. Give the reporter the truthful answers she wants. But for maximum results for your district, sandwich the answer around your own agenda. State the message you want to get out, regardless of the question. Get in your points about an issue early in the conversation, because questions that give you the opportunity you want may never be asked.

2. Repeat your points frequently.

It may sound silly in normal conversation to repeat points you've already made once or twice. But in dealing with reporters, repeating your points makes your message more likely to be reported. It is less likely that your message will be left on the cutting room floor if you sprinkle your answers with messages that make your case. In dealing with print reporters, restating your points makes it easier for your reporter to get an accurate quotation.

3. Don't repeat a reporter's negative comments or accusations in your answers.

Avoid the practice of perpetuating negative statements. Never repeat a reporter's accusations in your answers – otherwise you will end up being the one quoted with negative words coming out of your mouth. How often does a reporter quote his own questions? Seldom, if ever. Example: A reporter asks, "Why are you wasting money on buying new trucks for your maintenance crews?" Wrong answer: "We are not wasting money on new trucks. We need new trucks." Better answer: "Our trucks are 8 years old and each has logged a half million miles. We are at a point where it's cheaper for us to add new trucks to the fleet than to continue repairs on our old ones."

4. Be early with good news; late in the week with bad news.

For more news coverage, plan newsworthy events for Monday. It's early in the week and there are fewer news stories developing. Release bad news late Friday where there is less likelihood that a reporter can collect negative reaction quotes and when the weekend will help people forget the bad news. Friday's evening news attracts fewer viewers.

5. Never hide bad news or damaging facts.

Open and frank conversations with reporters over time build credibility. If there is a damaging fact or figure in your closet, you can be sure it will come to light at some point. There is practically nothing a reporter can't find out by asking enough people, searching records or invoking the Public Records Act. When it comes to bad news, the best defense is a good offense.

6. Going off the record will come back to haunt you.

First, you can't necessarily trust that your remarks will be off the record. Second, once the comments are out, a reporter can easily find a public record or another source who will talk about the very subject you want to hush up.

7. Help reporters do their jobs.

A reporter must file a story. If you stall in giving information, you just make life harder and do yourself no favors. The story will happen without you. Get the reporter the facts and information requested. Step away from a meeting to take a few questions. Tell the reporter your work situation, so she can adjust her schedule and expectations accordingly. The story will happen whether you like it or not. When you help; you are a hero. When you resist, you create suspicions and ill feelings.

8. Never guess.

You can't be expected to know everything. When you don't know an answer, say so, but promise to find out. Then get back with the correct information. If you speculate, you'll be cited as a source for bad information and then look silly or incredible. Give reporters an approximate time when they can expect a follow-up call from you. That helps them plan around their own deadlines. It also gives you time to dig out other facts and nuances that may clarify an issue. Being able to talk to a reporter twice on one subject is a gift. Use it wisely.

Smiling on the Phone

D o you ever feel irritated when the phone rings? Do people in your district constantly go through a voice mail maze, only to be put on hold for several minutes by the receptionist? Perhaps you should take a look at the phone etiquette in your department, including your own feelings regarding callers. Remind yourself how to create goodwill, as well as improve your own post-phone call happiness through a few simple guidelines for talking on the phone.

1. Approach your telephone calls as an opportunity.
Think like a marketing executive. Train your staff to view calls differently, not as an intrusion, but as an opportunity to win favor. Imagine the goodwill you will engender within your community if 20 callers a day go

away thinking your department is the most helpful, most considerate and most cheerful they have encountered. In days when public education gets so many knocks, this is a more consistent and effective way of building trust and support than getting TV coverage or issuing annual reports. Ask your staff to tally how many callers they think they left happy and satisfied after a call. Then think about this: When people stop calling, they don't need you anymore.

2. Answer with the proper I. D.

Just as you expect callers to identify themselves, you should do the same – as soon as the call is answered. Often callers from within your community have no idea how your district is organized. Some wonder, "Have I called the right office?" So, in addition, you should state the name of your department and office. Such a practice saves time, makes callers comfortable and sets boundaries for the content of a conversation.

3. Answer quickly with adequate tools.

Phones should not ring more than twice. Never answer a phone without a pencil or pen. If you have to say, "Please wait while I find a pen," the caller knows you have not been serious about the content of the call. If you use computer software to track calls, that's fine, but you must be ready to use it when the call arrives.

For every call, write down the name of the caller immediately. Use phonetic spelling if necessary. Also, use the caller's name in the conversation. This lets the caller know that you are paying attention and that the caller is important to you. Use the name as you speak.

4. Smile when you talk.
This is the most common suggestion among telephone etiquette gurus, but the advice works. It's almost impossible to sound disagreeable when you have a smile on your face. Smiling doesn't mean being overly perky. Rather, a simple smile helps you sound warm, receptive and pleasant. Your students' parents, contractors, community members and vendors want a receptive voice on the phone. Give people what they want. Start with a smile.

5. Practice active listening.
You will save time and grief later by paying attention to the caller the first time through the conversation. That means not doing two things at the same time. To improve your concentration, mentally picture the other person on the line. Listen for ideas, not just words. Don't jump to conclusions. Sound involved by holding the telephone handset about one inch from your mouth to avoid being muffled or distant. Restate the caller's concerns, clarify the action required, and follow through

on promises and requests for information. It is almost always better to say, "Let me check and find out," than to simply tell a caller, "I don't know."

6. Practice conciliation, not obstruction.

When a person calls with a problem, he or she usually wants to achieve a resolution. Work to get the problem resolved. Practice empathy. Put yourself in the other person's position. If the caller suggests a course of action, avoid statements such as, "We can't do that." Instead, propose an alternative solution. Explain your limitations and agree to work toward a mutually satisfactory solution.

7. Transfer calls reluctantly and courteously.

Help each caller to the utmost degree possible. Transfer is a last resort. Use it only if you are sure you cannot help, not because you think the call is someone else's job. Transfer calls only if you are certain the caller will be able to get the help needed at the point of transfer. Tell the caller the name of the person to whom you are referring the call. If your system allows, stay on the call until the call is connected. If a caller has already been transferred twice, apologize; offer to take matters into your own hands by researching an issue, promising a call back or walking a message into another department.

8. Avoid placing calls on hold.

You are testing your reputation when you put a caller on hold. You almost always lose more goodwill than you gain. If you must use the hold button, tell the caller why. Ask for consent and wait for his or her answer. If the answer is no, find out what is needed and establish a time to call. When you place a call on hold, return with progress reports every half minute or so, and use the caller's name in your report.

Avoiding Negotiation Traps

We all negotiate at one time or another. Mastering negotiation skills can make this process much smoother for you, as well as help you obtain your primary goals. If you regularly are regularly involved in negotiations, it is even more important that you learn to avoid the following negotiation traps at all costs.

1. Not viewing negotiations as a two-way street.
Bargaining means being prepared to give something up. Whether you are negotiating a price with a vendor or a change order with a contractor, view your negotiations as a conference, not a lecture or an ultimatum. Even when you are in total control, you must let conversations and concessions move both ways. If you win now and

they lose, you will ultimately lose later. If it's not a two-sided process, don't bother to begin the bargaining in the first place.

2. Forgetting to exhibit "must-be-but" qualities.

Don't exhibit a one-sided personality. For every show of power, strength and knowledge, show a contrasting quality of humility, compassion and openness. These contrasting traits lay the foundation for dynamic human interaction that lead to win-win deals. So, for example, you must be compassionate, but indifferent. To negotiate effectively, you must be strong but vulnerable. You must be friendly, but aloof. Each quality has an opposite.

3. Losing your credibility through the back door.

Credibility strengthens your negotiating position. Every statement you make in negotiations must be true. Watch for tactics and statements that inadvertently hurt your credibility. For example, you set a deadline and nothing happens. You claim you are the final decision-maker yet can't get the deal approved. You say some issue is a "must-have" for your district, but you concede the point for a minor trade-off.

4. Treating your BATNA as your bottom line.

If you are experienced with non-adversarial bargaining, you know that a BATNA is your "best alternative to a negotiated agreement." A BATNA is what you could have had if you did not enter negotiations in the first place. Therefore, your bottom line for success in negotiations must be a higher and greater benefit to you. Otherwise, you've wasted your time going to the table.

5. Being threatened by time spent in negotiations.
The more time you spend across the table from a vendor, contractor or bargaining unit, the more investment and ownership that party has in reaching a successful conclusion. People want value and results to come from their time, even if they are not being paid. A person is more likely to compromise the longer he or she is involved with you. The time you spend is an investment in your desired outcome. Knowing that, don't fall victim yourself to making a deal simply because you want the process to be over.

6. Caring too much.
You must care, but not too much. The secret of power in reaching a negotiation goal is being able to walk away, if you need to, accepting your alternatives. Of course you are interested in the deal, but you have choices. Always enter negotiations with options. Know the options of the party across the table. Your strength puts you in a better bargaining position.

7. Not knowing the interests of your counterparts.

Even if they have told you outright, you must do the research to find out what interests the persons across the table have in the negotiations. Of course, they may be asking for a sale, but do they have quotas to make, bosses to please, and inventory to reduce? Knowing their interests helps you devise a solution that pleases both sides. Sometimes the solution is not in what is proposed at the table. Knowing a person's interests allows you to think out of the box and create solutions no one has yet proposed.

8. Throwing out round numbers.

Most pricing and economic proposals are somewhat arbitrary. Of course no one wants to lose money, but the fact is, there is room to wiggle in almost every quotation or proposal. Whether you are offering or countering, a round number sticks out and shouts that there is room for more concession. An odd number or fraction gives the appearance of some reasonable thought behind the proposition.

Reducing the Risk of Injuries

The incidence of employees affected by ergonomic problems continues to rise, even though research is readily available to show that the method of our work can lead to injuries What can be done in your office to eliminate office injuries?

1. Realize that ergonomics may not be the total answer.

A risk manager worked with a group to ensure excellent ergonomics. All work stations were ergonomically correct and adjustable. Problems persisted. The problem was the hiring process. Hire the staff person who is appropriate to the job and task. Spell out the qualifications necessary in job descriptions.

2. Group training in ergonomics may be inefficient.
Equipment work stations and tasks vary so much
from place to place that group training often becomes
too theoretical and does not apply. Decide whether
individual attention and ergonomic corrections at
individual work stations are more likely to correct real
problems.

3. Work with physicians and physical therapists.
Doctors and therapists must have information about the
functional capacity requirements of the job; if they do
not, they are making blind recommendations about a
person returning to work. The secret is communication.

4. Do your homework in investigating claims.
Why should office injury claims get less attention than,
say, automobile accidents by risk managers and safety
officers? Office injuries can turn out to be expensive.
Do your homework right away. That may mean
photographing work stations, taking measurements and
noting any information that may prove beneficial to your
case. Experience has shown that documented facts beat
anecdotal evidence in claims settlements.

**5. Choose the right keyboard configurations because
keyboards are your primary office tool.**
Research suggests that when the wrist deviates from

a neutral position, the likelihood of developing carpal tunnel syndrome increases. Carpal tunnel syndrome is the most common of repetitive strain injuries. Among the best keyboard solutions are a preset tiltdown system. Interestingly, popular fixed angle split keyboards with centered mouse balls do not provide the ergonomic benefits usually desired. Studies of the keyboards showed typing speed decreased almost five words per minute. Typing accuracy decreased about 2 percent, and video motion studies found no statistically significant differences for wrist extension and ulna deviation while typing.

Making Buses Even Safer

School buses already are among the safest modes of transportation. Here's how to make the ride even safer for the kids in your school district.

1. Build partnerships with local and state law enforcement.

If local police or deputies know your problems, they can help you solve them. If it's unlawfully passing on the left that's the problem, let them know. Have regularly scheduled meetings to note problems and actions needed.

2. Distribute bus rules more than once a year.

Ensuring on-board discipline is as effective in May as it is in September, remind riders and their parents of the riding rules more than just at the beginning of the year. A driver's attention needs to be on the road, not on the behavior of students behind.

3. Install on-board cameras and camera boxes.
Cameras protect both students and drivers. They provide an extra measure of accountability to all parties. It is not always necessary to have a camera in every bus. Roving cameras can be used, if you also install camera boxes. Only supervisors know which buses are monitored on a given day, but a real and present camera is always better.

4. Check on volume.
The National Transportation Safety Board found in one bus accident that on board noise prevented the driver from hearing an approaching train. Drivers need to be able to hear sirens, trains, and horns. Check on the location of bus radio and stereo speakers. Disable those immediately adjacent to a driver's head. Maintain a reasonably quiet bus.

5. Keep driver morale high.
The Insurance Institute for Highway Safety has found that poor driving is more often attributable to a driver's attitude than to skills or knowledge. Drivers need the reward and satisfaction they get from being part of an important team. Develop excellent communication

systems and programs for participation of drivers in issues that affect their jobs.

6. Put up a daily fight against complacency.

One rule ignored or one precaution overlooked can be deadly in transporting students. Granted, school bus transportation is one of the safest modes of transportation in the world. But one year 25 children died in accidents just in bus loading zones, and the bus was not necessarily at fault. Safety is the responsibility of all administrators and staff. Help drivers, mechanics and supervisors think as if they are transporting their own family. Follow every procedure every day.

7. Plan for bus replacement.

Many school districts are still using buses that pre-date now accepted safety standards. We still spot a couple buses that carry black and yellow plates from the 1960s. These buses are safe. But other buses are safer. If you do not have a plan for bus replacement, put one in place. If there is no plan, there will never be a good time to upgrade your fleet with modern and safer equipment.

Making Quick Calculations

S ometimes it is faster to do a calculation in your head or on paper than it is to grab a calculator and enter all the numbers. You'll save time and impress your associates using these math tips.

1. Multiplying any given number containing two digits by 11.

Add the two digits of the given number together and place them between the same two-digit number. For example, when multiplying 54 x 11, add the numbers five and four to get nine. Place nine between the five and the four that make up the number 54 and you get the correct answer of 594. The only difficulty you will experience is when the sum of the digits becomes a two-digit number itself. In those cases, increase the left hand digit by one, which has the effect of carrying. Take, for example, 97 x 11. Nine plus seven equals 16. Carry the 1 to the left digit of nine, making it 10. Then, insert the remaining number 6 between 10 and 7. The correct answer will be 1,067.

2. Squaring numbers that end in the number five.

You may occasionally run across a situation in which you have to multiply a number times itself. If the number ends in five, it's easy. Simply multiply the 10s digit by itself plus one, then append 25 to the result. In the example 85 x 85, take the 10s digit, which is eight. Add one to it. That becomes nine. Multiply nine times the original eight digit to produce 72. Append 25 the result and the correct answer is 7,225.

3. Multiplying numbers between 10 and 19.

Memorize this trick and you'll never need a calculator for simple multiplication for numbers between 10 and 19. You can use your head with three quick steps. First, add the last digit of either of two given numbers to the other whole number in the problem. Second, put a zero behind the result. Third, multiply the last two digits of both numbers and add to the result in step two. It is easier to follow if you use an example. Take 13 x 18. In step one, you add three to 18 to get 21. Adding a zero to the result makes 210. Hold that number aside. Next, multiply the last two digits of the original numbers (13 and 18), three and eight, to get 24. Add it to 210 to get the correct answer of 234.

4. Find 2.5 percent.

This percentage is commonly helpful in rounding, especially in estimating COLAs, inflation, or bracket creep on a salary schedule. Start with two digit numbers to practice, then move to larger numbers. If it is helpful for estimating, round your large numbers to two or three digits then add as many zeros as you need to match your millions. The steps simply are to divide your number in half two times and move your decimal point one place to the left. Thus, 86 divides once to 43 and a second time to 21.5. Move the decimal point to the left and the answer is 2.15. Want to see that again? This time take a $28,993,444 certificated payroll. Round to 29. Halving the result is 14.5. Dividing again gets you to 7.25. Move the decimal point to the left and the answer is .725. Since you were estimating millions, restore six decimal places. Your 2.5 percent raise will cost you approximately $725,000.

5. Multiplying by 33 1/3 and taking thirds.

This may take some quick pencil strokes, but practice will make this trick even easier to do in your head. To multiply any given number by 33 1/3, simply take the given number, append two zeros and divide by 3. Thus, in the example, 483 x 33 1/3, the given number 483 becomes 48,300. Dividing by three results in 16,100. Going the other direction, you can also calculate percentages or thirds by simply moving the decimal point two places to the left. Thus, one third of 483 is 161, leaving the tiny fractions aside.

Dealing with Stress

There are many factors that contribute to individual stress levels, including difficult coworker relations, personal problems, and feelings of job insecurity. Some stressors can be avoided or minimized, while others must be attacked daily. When you find yourself in a stressful situation, it's best to have a strategy in place to minimize the adverse effects of the stress.

1. Anticipate stress-related events and circumstances. Work is not play. Your day is probably not going to be fun and games. That's why you get paid. You can expect activities, circumstances, deadlines and pressures that produce stress. The key is to anticipate and plan counter strategies to stress-causing conditions. To get a handle on your situation, keep a "quick-jot" journal on your desk.

2. Know what you can control, then plan.

After anticipating and evaluating, distinguish between those stressors you can control and those that you cannot. Where you have control, practice prevention. Where you have no control, practice responses, especially in dealing with coworkers. Your success in preventing and responding requires a written plan with goals. If you don't write something down, you will not be as accountable to yourself. Set short- and long-term goals. Identify strategies. Reward yourself at important milestone steps.

3. Identify stress-busters that work for you.

When stressors threaten, know what prevention and counter measures work for you. For example, if your boss loads you up with unmanageable work, can you "reframe" the situation? Can you change a negative into a positive by breaking the work into pieces and further delegating parts? If you become angry, can you practice a "walk-away?" If you are hit with criticism, can you do a "behind-the-words analysis," objectively separating out your hurt feelings? Visit a web site or pick up a book to discover strategies that work for you.

4. Check on environmental stressors.

It's enough that people and work cause stress. Don't let simple environmental problems add to stress unnecessarily. Is your keyboard at the right height? Do you have a comfortable chair? Are you sitting under an air conditioning vent? Is there enough light at your work station? Most of these problems are easily solved. Take care of them so they don't add more stress on top of the relationship, policy and work issues which take greater effort to control.

5. Practice regular relaxation techniques.

Are you too busy to take breaks? If yes, you may be adding to your stress and working less efficiently than you could. If you don't want to hang out in the break room, take a walk around the building. During a tense meeting, take a few quiet, deep breaths. Relax your jaw and practice on-the-spot relaxation just prior to public speaking. Tense after building a complicated spreadsheet? Quickly look away; practice relaxing all your muscles groups, starting from your head and moving to your toes. Then make sure you regularly get a good night's sleep.

6. Avoid chemical stressors.

Your body is like a machine. Your diet gives it the chemicals and fuels it needs to work. Eat in balance and you will feel better. That means eating just the right combination of proteins, fats and carbohydrates. Fit people handle stress better. Avoid caffeine which drains the body of vitamin B. Less caffeine and alcohol mean better sleep and more overall energy. The nicotine in tobacco may relax you for a brief spell, but it ends up raising your heart rate and adding to biological stress.

Preparing for Cuts

G ood economies don't last forever. Do you have a plan for cuts when the time arrives? Will encroachments eventually force you to save money in core programs? Are employee contracts forcing a second look at expenses? Do you just want to run the most efficient operation possible? Use these tips as you begin to survey the potential for downsizing.

1. Cut out work, not necessarily jobs.

Lay off gardeners and the grass still grows; you haven't eliminated the work. Don't arbitrarily cut jobs as a cost-cutting measure. Instead, first examine work that can be abolished because it is not legally required, is not contributing to efficient operations or is not contributing to the education product. Then consolidate and eliminate positions accordingly. Management guru Peter Drucker estimates that up to one-third of clerical and control functions are unnecessary.

2. Document non-production immediately.

When times are good, don't put up with employees who are non-productive or incompetent. Document performance now. Counsel these employees out or use due process to end their employment with you. When tough financial times arrive, you can't rush through a series of evaluations and hope to be successful. Cultivate an excellent staff now, and you will be able to survive cutbacks better during hard times.

3. Use machines and software to simplify and replace laborious tasks.

Bar coding replaces myriad clerical tasks. High volume copiers require less operating skill than an offset press. Duplicators use a simpler technology than copiers, providing lower costs per copy. Software can replace many districts' time sheet and position control systems. TV cameras provide more visibility for security than patrols. Voice recognition software replaces dictating to secretaries. There are plenty of new ways to use machines and technology as an efficient alternative to human labor.

4. Analyze extra assignment pay and release time.

Run a report on extra assignment pay and release time. You will be amazed at why you are paying people to leave the classroom or what extra duties are being performed around the district. If it is "extra," does it support student achievement or add to more efficient operations?

5. Don't skimp on training.

If you cut back on training, you are likely to cut back on efficiency. We know of one instance where one hour of training on new software was provided to employees. When it came to implementation, the department lost days of work because the training of clerical staff was inadequate. Training usually ends up saving you time and money.

6. Shop around – again – for big-ticket expenses.

You have probably already shopped around for big expenses in utility and phone service, legal counsel, Medicaid claims, and computer programming. In today's competitive and deregulated market, it pays to shop more often and to negotiate harder.

Discussing Ballot Propositions

With ballot measures and propositions always on the horizon, it pays for school administrators to review proper protocol with regard to how they spend time and school funds in connection with an election.

1. State the facts fully.

In preparing a school district analysis of the impact of a ballot measure, use your best professional judgment of what the impact of the measure will be, both positive or negative. Be fair in reviewing both the good and bad aspects of the measure. Stipulate in your analysis whether your scope of review is comprehensive or limited to the financial and operational aspects of the initiative.

2. Don't editorialize.

It is OK to say in your best judgment that the effect of an initiative would be deleterious or beneficial in certain respects as long as you are fair. However, do not use your analysis to editorialize that "this measure should be defeated" or "we need to support this measure."

3. Well-crafted resolutions are OK.

A board of education may adopt a resolution in support or opposition to a measure, but the language should be factual in nature. Let the facts speak for themselves, and resist the urge to tell your voters how they should vote.

4. Factual information can be distributed.

If you have done a fair and professional job on your analysis, share and distribute your work to employees and community groups.

5. Limit your role in public appearances.

If you are called upon by a community group to speak about an initiative or measure, limit your remarks to a fair and impartial representation of the facts.

6. Do not use district equipment.

Fax machines, email, phones and copiers must not be used to communicate for or against a measure. Make this rule clear to your staff.

Making Meetings More Effective

At times it feels like it is impossible to get anything done as a result of the profusion of meetings taking up our time. If meetings are planned and run well, our time would be much better spent.

1. Ask if you really need a meeting.

Do you feel as if you have so many meetings producing new work that you never have time to do the work? You are not alone. The next time you are tempted to have a meeting, ask yourself, "Is a meeting really necessary?" The answer is no if 1) you have made the decision and just want a rubber stamp; 2) you can't get the right decision makers together; and 3) phone calls and emails are likely to give you the result you want.

2. Plan ahead because meetings are too expensive to hold without proper preparation.

Preparing means making the goal of the meeting clear ahead of time to all participants. You have failed if someone asks, "Why am I here?" Prepare the room ahead of time. Publish an agenda or describe the topic on paper. Cabinet and staff meetings should have an agenda, but many do not. Leave one spot open for late-breaking items, but never purposely surprise your colleagues with a bomb-like topic. Start on time or you will always start late.

3. Participants must agree upon or understand the meeting process.

Is it a democracy? What are the ground rules? What roles does each person play? Who is the recorder? Does the facilitator get to engage in the discussion? Is candor welcome and rewarded? When is consensus reached? Is consensus necessary? Will the meeting produce a decision, a recommendation, or merely produce a report? Make the process clear. Better yet, establish a district culture on how meetings are run.

4. By definition, meetings should be interactive.

Meetings are not lectures or sermons. Everyone should have a role and purpose. Silence isn't the golden rule of meetings, so speak up and contribute to the group.

Facilitators need to watch the group. Talkative types are innocently oblivious to the fact that others in the room are trying to talk but keep getting cut off. Bosses and facilitators should not be so dominant that their voice and opinions quiet others, who may have new perspectives and different views.

5. Establish ground rules for decision-making.

It is often tempting to make decisions by voting, thus speeding up the yes or no process. It is more important, however, to reach a decision valued by most, if not all participants. Encourage members to brainstorm issues up for discussion, then analyze the pros and cons of each issue. Once the facets of the decision are clear, it is best to decide by consensus, which maximizes the buy-in from meeting participants. If consensus is not possible, make the decision by compromise or by voting. Avoid whenever possible making decisions by dictatorship, or as a result of the silence of other members.

6. One person must lead every meeting, even if by default.

Equal rank and collegiality are fine, but every meeting needs a person to enforce the ground rules. A cabinet meeting without the superintendent or facilitator present can quickly turn into a bar brawl. Telling your staff to meet and work it out will amount to a cat-and-dog fight. A meeting leader must be appointed to protect participants from personal attacks and promote open conversation.

Increasing Lunch Sales

Are you interested in increasing student participation in your lunch and cafeteria program? To help build sales among students, take a look at what some schools have done and achieved success.

1. Change your department's mind set.

You are more than a lunch program. Every employee must understand that service and sales are as important as simply delivering a food product. Yes, you are there to make sure students get fed, but this should not be a get-it-done-and-over-with activity. Food service is not an entitlement, but rather a sales and service business. Even the youngest students must feel like customers who are served and valued. Instill every person in the department with a sense of responsibility to increase participation – especially by making the buying experience as fun and pleasant as possible. No student should go without seeing a smile and receiving a warm greeting.

2. Work the lines.

This means not only eliminating wait time, but also making the most of students' time and attention while they are in line. This is the chance to promote *a la carte*. Publicize tomorrow's menu specials as well. Do you have a variety of signage that can be read from all points in the line? Have you considered TV monitors or Power Point displays? How about games and contests in line? Moveable sandwich boards and a sample display of food options at the end of the line will increase student interest as well.

3. Use your cashier as a sales rep.

Not only should you have enough cashiers to make the lines run quickly, but you also want enough cashiers so they have sufficient time to help make extra sales. "Would you like a frosty vanilla shake with that sandwich?" "How about a homemade chocolate chip cookie today?" These invitations work. They work even better if you offer a choice in the same sentence. "Would you like a bottle of juice or a carton of chocolate milk?" Track your daily sales to judge the impact suggestions make on student populations that have discretionary change in their pockets. Restaurant personnel are trained to offer suggestions before a customer ever orders or inquires. To sell is to serve.

4. Don't depend solely on the menu.

Won't it be a wonderful day when the teacher who takes the lunch count also promotes the menu and specials as successfully as an experienced waiter? In the meantime, exploit as many options as possible outside the standard menus. All the rules of promotion apply. Schools have used balloons, hot dog characters, walking vegetables, sampling and contests to promote their products. Selling food is a show business. You need props. Consider table tents, pictures of your students eating your food, and of course, smells of cinnamon and freshly baked goods.

5. Treat parents like customers, too.

Parents are as much the customer as students. They want a personal benefit before they will part with their money to participate in your program. Communicate with parents and get them excited about convenience, balanced nutrition and great prices. Are you involved in open house and back-to-school night? Do you design your menus and notices to get the attention of busy parents? Have you found ways to reach parents besides the take-home menu, for example, by using radio public service spots, the Internet and school marquees?

Dealing with Bomb Threats

In this era of multiple bomb threats in public areas, including schools, are you prepared to handle a crisis situation? Develop your response plan.

1. Have a specific plan in place to deal with bomb threats.

If you already have your plan in place, it is a good idea to pull out that section and send it out to administrators for an extra review periodically. How often are your administrators reviewing their safety and security plans anyway? Probably less than once a year. It is particularly important to share the bomb threat portion of the plan with people who answer the telephone. Having a plan for a bomb threat helps your staff deal with the threat in a rational and calm way. It minimizes the risk to personal safety and facilities. It also makes them feel better knowing there is a plan if something should happen.

2. Review your plan ahead of time with local law enforcement.

One of the main problems with any school plan is that your plan will not mesh with the way local law enforcement officers and agencies will come in and deal with the problem. They will ignore your plan over their good judgment on the scene. It is better to know something of their procedures ahead of time. Coordinate with them, or your plan may end up being useless when the problem occurs.

3. Know your sites better than potential bombers.

Your staff knows their sites better than anyone. Identify potential hiding places ahead of time. Minimize those areas' potential to store or hide any kind of devices. List those spots so law enforcement can search them. But understand that a bomb can be placed anywhere – in open areas and well as enclosed areas. Don't think you are immune because you don't have lockers, unlocked cabinets and alcoves.

4. Put questions by your phone.

The FBI suggests nine questions to ask a person who threatens a bomb: When is the bomb going to explode?

Where is it right now? What does it look like? What kind of bomb is it? What will cause it to explode? Did you place the bomb? Why? What is your address? What is your name?

5. Train staff to listen beyond the answers.
Staff who receive bomb threats should be prepared to listen beyond the answers given by the caller and pay attention to the voice and background noises. Was the voice male or female, with an accent, disguised, well spoken or foul? Was the caller's emotional state calm, angry, rushed or nervous? What background noises did you hear? A tardy bell, students talking, playground sounds, restaurant noises, street sounds, music, motors, machinery, static? Create a worksheet to accompany your plan that a staff member could use to record such information.

6. Follow your plan, if you actually find a suspicious object.
Don't hem and haw about whether you should implement your plan if you find a suspicious object or a bomb. Your plans will tell you how to immediately evacuate a building. No one on your staff should ever touch or move the object. The plan will suggest certain immediate mitigations you can undertake while law enforcement arrives, such as opening doors and windows

to minimize fragmentation damage and establishing clear zones within 300 feet of the threat.

Assessing Decision Risk

Assessing risk is a fundamental component of sound decision making. Your tolerance for risk and the potential consequences of a decision affect which course you take. But are you assessing potential risks both objectively and broadly? Here are some tips to put risk tolerance into a proper perspective.

1. Avoid temptations to manipulate statistical outcomes.

Your natural inclination to be fiscally conservative may prompt you to lower or raise the statistical base upon which you are fashioning your decision. While protecting you personally, this inserts an entire tone of pessimism into your decision making. Your approach is likely to be overly cautious. Resources needed for your plan may be tied up in an unnecessary holding pattern. Be honest with yourself. Give wide publicity and scrutiny to your assumptions. Assess your risk base on a reasonable foundation, then make your decision.

2. Don't pay undue attention to the negative side of a risk chart.

Just as you may be tempted to be overly cautious in establishing a statistical base, business officials can give undue attention to the negative consequences of a potential decision just because they are negative. Put both the likely negative and positive outcomes on a decision making scale. Negative outcomes do not necessarily weigh more. If they did, we would never have traveled to the moon. Positive outcomes can be achieved even if a few of the negative consequences come into play. If you have reached your goal, you are successful. New goals can be set to mitigate any negative fallout.

3. Check personal optimism against empirical reasoning.

A project can have a "sexy" feel. There may be personal benefits or rewarding career advances if you succeed on a project. The enthusiasm you have heading down a decision path must be checked by rational facts and risk assessment. Candidly answer the question, "If I had no personal involvement in this project, would I perceive the degree of risk differently?" If yes, factor out your involvement and then make the decision.

4. Be prompt in assessing complex or difficult questions.

Postponing risk assessment on a difficult project does not make the job easier. Usually, it makes the decision worse because delays add a new layer of money problems, politics and discontent to assess. If the task appears daunting – such as a big decision to close a school or to pursue imminent domain – chart out with pen and paper risk assessment in the various component parts. Risk in the smaller parts can then be connected to a whole, so that decisions can be made objectively.

Getting Copyright Right

Sometimes neglected both in the creation of materials and the copying of other's work, copyright laws affect school districts as much as they do individuals and corporations. It pays to study copyright laws and guidelines. Begin by using these tips.

1. Afford yourself extra protection.
All works are automatically copyrighted the moment they are put in some tangible form – even if in electronic form. However, a writer is afforded extra protection if he or she includes an official copyright notice that includes the copyright symbol, the year of copyright and the name of the owner of the copyright. Even as a district, you will need this official notice in court to help prove

"willful" misuse of your materials. Pay the fees and use the online registration process to protect your work.

2. Clarify who the copyright owner is ahead of time.
If a team of bus drivers meets as a committee to compile a new safety manual, the district is the owner of the material and the copyright. The manual is a work for hire, as would be an in-house math textbook created by a committee of teachers. Likewise, an outside group – such as a county office or a university – subsidizing the expenses of a team to create a work could lay claims to copyright ownership. If you are creating anything on company time, the product is "work for hire" and belongs to your employer. A school district employer cannot return rights to you without the transfer being a gift of public funds. If you are creating something on your own time that is related to your job, do not use any district computers or resources. Get a written understanding ahead of time about the ownership of your work and the district's use of that work.

3. Make use of expired copyrights and public domain materials.
Copyrights do not last forever. Copyrights are guaranteed by the U.S. Constitution to "promote the progress of science and useful arts." Anything copyrighted before 1978 has a maximum copyright of

75 years. When a copyright expires, it is said to be in the public domain. For some older works, such as a Shakespearian play, a district may retype or download the play and publish the work itself in its own print shop, perhaps cheaper than it could buy it from a publisher. Works created by the federal government are in the public domain, cannot be copyrighted and can be reproduced without permission.

4. Beware of violating letter, email and web page copyrights.

Just because someone sent you a letter does not mean that you can copy that letter to 100 of your friends or publish it in the district newsletter. The prose of an original letter is protected just as much as the prose of a novel. Thus, be careful about copying opinions from an attorney, unless the work qualifies as a "work for hire," which in most cases it does. Email is considered the same as a letter and is protected. So are web pages, even if the page fails to include an official copyright notice.

5. Be fair with special privileges granted to schools.

Schools have special privileges – although by case law and not by statute – when it comes to making copies. Since they are special, you should take pains to enforce the minimal requirements for copying in your district or someday risk losing the privilege. Teachers can make a copy of an illustration, a book chapter, a short story of up to 2,500 words, or a poem of up to 250 words. He or she can also make one copy for each student in the class. However, the copying must be spontaneous. That is, it cannot be dictated or suggested by administrators. It cannot be planned so far in advance that it would have been possible to write for permission. It cannot be used systematically over many terms, years or semesters. However, "spontaneous" does not mean the teacher has to be standing in front of the copy machine when he makes the decision. The teacher can still send the item to a centralized district print shop for duplication and be within the guidelines. In addition, the teacher must include the full copyright notice on the copies being made. Failure to do so exposes the teacher and the district to possible lawsuits.

Tracking the Economy

Without being an economist, you can get a quick overview of the economy by studying a few reports and indices. Before you make long term commitments, take a look at economic conditions.

1. Review the industrial sectors with the Purchasing Managers' Index (PMI).

The Institute for Supply Management tracks the levels of industrial orders and creates a composite of industrial conditions. The break point is 50. When the index is below 50, conditions are contracting. Three months of decline indicate an economic slowdown has begun.

2. Home sales can portend recession or signal growth.
The level of home sales is a clear indicator of consumer demand. Although sometimes volatile, this index of both housing completions and turnover is influenced both by income levels and mortgage rates.

3. Don't be tricked by GDP.
The Gross Domestic Product is the sum of total economic activity in the country. When it moves up, that's generally considered good. But don't be tricked, because rapid increases in inflation can pollute the figures. Real GDP adjusts for inflation. GDP is issued quarterly. Three consecutive negative figures constitute the definition of recession.

4. People spend when they feel good.
Consumer spending is a driving force of the economy, making up as much as two-thirds of the gross domestic product. The more optimistic consumers are, the more they spend. The Conference Board reports an index of consumer confidence monthly in arrears, as the percentage of consumers feeling more optimistic less those feeling less optimistic.

5. Visit your state department of finance.
All state budgets are based on estimated revenues. Make it a habit to review monthly revenue reports online.